REQUIEM FOR THE LIVING

A COLLECTION OF POEMS

Jeanette Bresson Ladegaard Knox

ISBN: 978-0-9996208-2-3

Requiem For The Living/Knox-1st ed.

1. Poems. 2. Poetry. 3. Verse.

4. Knox

Cover painting; The Last Fires by Stephen Whittaker

website: http://www.sgwhittaker.com

NFB Publishing/Amelia Press
<<<>>>
119 Dorchester Road
Buffalo, New York 14213
For more information please visit
nfbpublishing.com

To *you*,
For all you sat in motion

The poem is [...] a vortex that snatches us away. Not gradually, but...suddenly... [...]. We are forcefully drawn into a conversation.

- Martin Heidegger

The Fundamental Concepts of Metaphysics

Perhaps all the dragons in our lives are princesses who are only waiting to see us act, just once, with beauty and courage. Perhaps everything that frightens us is, in its deepest essence, something helpless that wants our love.

- Rainer Maria Rilke
Fear of the Inexplicable

Contents

The unity of life and death

Do not make me speak badly of my death

I will not hear of it

For its harvest is serene

Pure and naked

Awakenings

The deepest connection to life I know

Sure I tussle

It is a beautiful human flaw

But the dying in me

Is a song

That wants to sing itself

A requiem for the living

Walk the walk

Behind every step

Lurks a new beginning

Every day is a day of commitment

Remembering the thin membrane

Between left

And right

The virginity of the day

The virginity of the day

Stares at us

Afresh

Beaming

With a craving

Exclaiming

Consume me!

Connection

My world wraps its arms and legs around you

I drink from the fruits of your glowing skin

Sink into the songs and shadows in your eyes

And surrender to the riddle of love, love, love

Where the two of us

Dissolve toxic schemes and shoulds and

Transform into servants of the rippling pure stream

That runs through all great and glorious things

Love is a virtue

For its realization stems from the cradle of action

And resonates through exploration and excellence

Love is noble

For it seeks not its own

But the well-being of the beloved

Love is courageous

For it makes a leap of faith

Amidst the brutality of life

Love is wise

For even when it is broken

It sings songs of passion

You burst like a star

You burst like a star within me
And light up a universe unknown
Of enigmatic and concentrated reality

You flow in my bloodstream like an endless river
Setting all things in motion
And entering into places no words have frequented before

You spread your roots into the depth of my heart
Plant there a garden with fruits and flowers
To the delight of my senses

You show me the light, you show me the dark
And the grey boundary that separate the two
Like the one between a man and a woman

You carry my breath gently upon your tongue
Allowing life to happen
And a partnership in this flawed and overwhelming existence of ours

You tell me from one amateur to another:
Surrender to the most difficult of all tasks
To love the other, another, one another

When holding someone's heart

It is no small matter

When holding someone's heart

In your hands

Do you know

That you carry

Your humanity

On your sleeves

For you hold, in fact

The very thing

That makes everything

Live

Prelude to an embrace

I kiss the forehead of the sweet thought of you
Hum your name like a sonnet
In the name of delight, desire and dread

Our experiences of life mingle
Like waves on the ocean wide
Our secret looks of longing twinkle
Like shooting stars in the skies

I wonder, I wonder as I wander, do you wonder – why
Our hands fumble
Our tongues tumble
Waiting for the grace of an embrace

A chorus of past cries roaring silently
Between us
The old odor of hurt
Though our bodies are drawn and our beings burn to cohere

We take up residence on the rainbow but thirst for matters of reality
And mourn the loss of opportunities that we let pass by
As we defy a world not of our making

Unveiled

I was shipwrecked on the sea of pure thought
Intoxicated by the consolation
Of living among unicorns and leprechauns
Shielded from breathing the air of real time

As the anchor of your being
Descended, descended
To the bottom of my heart
Without warning
Unknowingly
Unclosed me
Unclothed me
Made me bow to the grace of your hands
And sent me on a sobering journey
To the bittersweet experience of reality

Stripped of the mirages of imagination
Marked by the delight and terror of emotions
I live hopefully
In the uncertain forecast of the present

Enemy of love's orchard

The voice of your heart beaten to silence

In the cemetery of childhood

I sense the texture of your vulnerability

Beneath the years of mindful escape

You, mourner of a heart buried under leaves of pain

- Loneliness and bitterness await

Walk away, walk away, I heard you whisper

To the cry of my soul's request:

Let us water your orchard

Bring the hope of light to the fields of drought

Walk away, walk away, I heard you whisper

- but turn around when the future is near

Farewell

Hope breathes through lungs of another nature
Beyond reason, logic and will
The daughter of dreams, the mother of being

But - O hope - you spin me in whirlwinds of deception here
Call on me to an island that does not want to be found
- Set sail to the hope of him, set sail, set sail

While I am not looking
You blow back to shore
- The mind has little wind amidst forces of nature

But you and I must separate so that my heart can brake
And resurrect to the dawn of a new day
- Kneel to what appears before my eyes

I bid you farewell, I beg you
While the leaves of autumn fall in tremor as death nears
Fare well

You look at me from the corner of my eye

You left your fingerprints on the story of me

I carry them with me wherever I go

My secret treasure of tattoos

Pleasure and pain

The world is better for it

Within, you rest

Though a tempest reigns through me

Within, you rest

Though I wander through my nights' restless thoughts

Within me

You write a book for me to read

About the lessons I have learned

And the trail of choices to be made on the way

The house of Phoenix

I have wept so many times

In your absence

And still laid in a bed of

Lilies and lavender

Blossoming in the backyard

I have heard you sing

How you sweetened my world

And granted me a rebirth

While you perished in golden ashes

Resurrecting somewhere else

You need not grow in my garden

For me to house you in my heart

Ode to sorrow

Sorrow carved its way through my bones

As I looked up and out

Little did I know

That it carved a tunnel

To my heart

And the song

I must learn to sing

Kintsugi

When you broke my heart

And the damage was done

I explored wondrous places

Among fields of tears

Discovered cracks

That contained solid gold

I carry myself as a vase

Of broken glass

Pieced together by light

I am

Whole

Gloriously imperfect

Weeping willow

When you are a weeping willow like me
There is no sense in sweet talking the rain
She has her own design
Her command governs my growth

Living through nights of terror
My roots ache
Eager to grow and a stranger to patience
I murmur from underneath the grass

Pebbles of water enter me
At odd hours
Putting unexpected changes
In motion

They fall like messages
From a great beyond
And a hidden within
I offer myself to them

When I can

A world of words

Words exist like the moles peeking out from beneath the soil
Like the eagle scouting for prey
The olive tree in the field of olive trees
And the magnolia flower releasing its scent
Into the world of perception, reception, conception

Words heal by their very sound
Sweep into the darkest wounds
With balsam and caresses of light
Or spark animosity in hearts who rather
Clothe the world in categories and calamity

Words matter when it matters
In the haunted greenhouse
Of life
Where stories can make
Or break a season

Words inhabit roles
Designed for them by
The greatest playwright of them all: Imagination
Thrown into the world as webs of meaning
Enunciate, propagate, impregnate virgin sand

Words unfold
The millions of folds of reality
Balancing scales of belonging
Humble keepers of keys
To other disclosive horizons
On life's way

Ceasing to hear
The bells of melancholia
Playing tunes throughout the land
Of grand paradoxical truths
On life's stoney way
Numbs us to believe
That the wrinkles on our soul
Can be ironed flat:
The pathologization of
The natural chaos of being
Here

I, poiesis

I am a metaphor
Filling blood vessels
With the wilderness of
Imagination and passion

I am a metaphor
Breathing air into
The dissonance between
Idea and reality

Adventures of drinking water from a vase
Or stinging credos with dread
The enchanted play of molding clay
Disclosing newly born texts and textures
Living on the edge of uncertainties
Revelations float in a sea of paint
Stroking a canvas with unpredictability
And handmade precision

I am a metaphor
Perspiring stories
Through the skin in the sun
The whole condensed in imagery

Having gone through experience
All the way to the end

Sculptures of thought

Smitten by the claim breathing has on me
Yet intimidated by the sublimity of
Things being timely and timeless

My pen hides
In a hand full of unknown variables
Equations fit not a single body

Out of the mud, words creep
Slowly, timidly, slowly, slowly
Onto the paper like a beaten dog

Say it
Say what cannot be said
Say it anyway

Sculptures of thought
On a pilgrimage
Endless

Endlessly mystified

Confession

For thousands of years

I have stretched out my life in questioning

The flowing rivers and the uttered words

The sparkling moonbeams and the tender touch

I live in the floating of meanings

Transformed by the melting of experience on my skin

And moved by transcendence in the making

I confess

I am still wondering

What this whole thing is about

I am dazzled

I am dazzled by this:

There is no deception or lie

No sham or evasion

Of any sort

In mortality

There is but honesty

Inspiration

In the daily dailying I sometimes hear in the distance

A solemn chant

It is the making of a thought in my mind

In the drifting of time, it drops down

From its orbiting infinitude

And settles in

The world recreated

I am the one

Who illuminated the dark sky by rubbing two flint stones together

I am the one

Who drew steppe bisons and human hands in the cave of Altamira

I am the one

Who laid each brick and wooden beam of the White Horse Temple

I am the one

Who directed the paint Jackson Pollock splashed on canvas

I am the one

Who blows freshness into every exchange

I am the one

Who mirrors the leading edge of consciousness

I am the spirit you inhale

When eyes are wide open and

You exhale the world

Time after time

I am your sister, your brother, your cousin

All your life

You have heard the sound of me in you

I am as soft and rough as water flowing

Yet, you still have to go into the river

On your own

You are the one

You are the one

The rhapsody of the generations

We are all involved with the radiance of the daffodil

Engaged to the water that throws itself off the cliff

Married to the growing grass beneath our feet

All things are stretched out

Between strings on a lyre

The murmuring of life revealing its secrets

In an enchanting score for earth's offspring

We are all disfigured by the falling of apples

And asked to kneel before the tree of life

The rhapsody of the generations

Unpronounceable

When dialogue flourishes among voices

It perishes too

For at the very moment of its blossom, its own imperfection

- The cliffs of the land of language

Announces itself

When desires between two people melt to merge

Comprehension and control melt too

Mortal hearts are moved by inexplicable things

- The implosion of reason

Taken to a precious level of consciousness

Why waste our mind on matters of mystery

When no reasoned final word can be drawn from the history of man

The fragrance of human knowledge and emotion

- Wisdom's valley

Consists of the flowers born out of creativity and courage

The unpronounceable

A calling from inside a poem

And inside the universe

- The blessing of breathing questions

Imagination intercepts the real of real as it shapes the world

Cave paintings

Reality resides in caves

Of memories and expectations

Carved by imagination

Offering the mind

An intangible world

Of fulfilling presence

Life is a vocation
Without purpose
Other than living
In gratitude

Life is an honor
Without medals
Calling us
To the occasion

Life is a song
Without a written verse
In constant pursuit
Of fine tuning

Life is a mortality
Without mercy
Aspiring to faith
Among mortals

Beyond daydreaming

I travel, I travel
Joyfully beyond my experience
To a euphoric world of make belief
Where the puzzles of life fall into place
And ideals overrule the ticking of the clock

But one day when
I came back from my excursions
My homeland had been remodeled
My stained couch stood as a forest of sequoia trees
My cracked ceiling clouded by the tiniest raindrops

I peeled off the bark
Dug in the moist grass on the floor
I asked every person around
Can you see the anatomy of me?
Have I lost my visitation rights to my soul?

Glaring

Life glares at me from beyond time

It throws crumbs of poetry at my feet

Breathes through me as words fall from the sky

To embrace my hungry soul

Uplifted by what life's glaring can create

In the silence of my deepest nights

I cry out in longing

I have plenty of room within to hold more

I lay no claim but the grace of life's glaring

Is it too much to ask?

The pendulum

As I walk through the dale of my day
Life blows me in rhythmic oscillations
I brush the fiery fear of the unknown
Hanging in the clouds gathering above my head
I turn around and am stroked by the smiling sun
Waiting in anticipation in the distance
Clashing aromas of the heart embrace
Wondrously moving back and forth, back and forth

Passing through dense visions standing tall and prosperous
Tears drop like soft rain as I cross the rocky stream
I ask the skies how sighs can harbor bliss
One minute and boredom the next
I carry a habitat within and no map but my nose
From creation to ashes, I lend myself to a drama
Wearily moving back and forth, back and forth

In the equation of life
Fulcrum seems to be how
To rest with moving opposites
O how the world is a blur

The disquietude of silence

Silence drops like a drop of water

The whisper that tickles my ear while the galaxy turns

The winter frost on the lake of ancient myths

How intelligent that life soaks up its alphabet in silence

Uneasy around the disquietude of silence as if faced with death

We seem to be creatures

With a keen inclination

To silence the tempestuous trolls that tramp within

The questions that labor through the centuries look stillborn

In an age of blastering instant constant noise

Perhaps we are making the world infertile

With our rhetoric of grandeur and our chatter and jabber and blather

Making silence an orphan waiting persistently to be adopted

By a single moment of doubt

From where questions on fire are hauled

And trolls tamed by the very soul that cultivated them

Silence is the greatest disclaimer of world orthodoxy

I wear my death inside out

I wear my death inside out
Like the picture in Dorian Gray

Blind in a dark room
Fleeing the human condition
At every opportunity available
To the mind of men
Art mirrors the reality
We unwillingly face in actuality

Do not speak of diseases or
Accidents or
Heartaches or
Natural disasters
Utter no name
I do not die because of it

Mortality
Is the cause of death

The axis of anxiety

The seed of anxiety was planted in the front yard of my early years

Fostering a landscape of melancholia

Fields of numbing worries

Floods of unsettling confusions

Eruptions of ruminating thoughts gone wild

Quivering by its scolding reverie - sacrificial fire

Dissolvent of matters of the mind

Subpoenas me at every given moment

Reality blown to pieces, puzzle lost

Estranging my eyes from my vision

Master of distortion

Heart's luminations gone dim, love lost

When anxiety hides beneath the plains of control

It destines me to be a soul in exile

To harvest its crop

I must taste it on my tongue

Let it caress my skin

Face the embodiment of the word

Or I will be blind to its messenger of truth

Be wrapped in chains - so I cannot move

Be wrapped in rust - so I cannot be moved

A prisoner – or freedom fighter

Nothing in the world is single

The poet said

But solitude

I said

Midnight in soul

It is dark here like outer space

Black holes swallow up entire worlds

Of light and laughter

The journey of every vibration is at a standstill

A place of no vision

A pulse madly looking for a heart

Left with nothing but tears to guide it

I close my eyes and long to sense how

To live with comets and asteroids

Hurry - my flesh is consumed by a fire of sorts

In the trances of my heart

Bullets are still fired

And I wonder

If the bleeding is like watering a plant

Or if I am bleeding to death

There will be rain

You will look at the hounding wind

- Blowing through time

- Scarring your face

And not know the person

Or the havoc that absorbs you

There will be rain

You will be lured into believing

That the stars are aligned and the path is straight

But words will break under the burden

Of unprecedented experiences

And ungovernable variables will creep into your compass

There will be rain

Life will speak to you in tongues

Have mercy 'cause it knows no other resource

Plant each language in the valley of your soul

And care for each of them

Like they were your children

There will be rain

You will be born an apprentice

You will die a guardian

- of the precious call of

Being that suffered within

Throughout

There will be more rain

The secret source

All

Moves to the sound of life

In the anticipation of death

Breaths whisper their song

To the fragile tone between

Here and there

But we do not rock the cradle

We hold our breath

Until the end

Imperfection creates
Longing
Belonging
Becoming

Beauty inconcise
Finitude confused
Attunement to truth
Atonement

Concealment
Conversation
Companionship
Consenting to imperfection

Moving into its own
Approaching, achieving – never arriving
The art of living
Imperfection

We marry solitude
The minute we enter the school of life
As a friend it encourages us to look within
And befriend the world in the courtyard

Life sends a bold request to inhabit us
And to endure the questions
That are calling on us
From far beyond our reach

In the infinite distance that exist between us
What we can hope for is companionship
Alone we travel a road void of a fixed destination
If we are lucky we flourish in the sunlight of the unresolved

We are never ripe for living
It takes a lifetime to learn the moves
Yet we are called upon to embody
The exigencies of the day

Pandora's box

There are many paradoxes in the world

How is it that the acceptance

Of mortality

Expands being

To a calling

Beyond comprehension

A gentle whisper ruminating

Not to install tremor and terror

Or to be a foreigner

It is like a child

Wanting to be noticed

Walking along side us

The passage (or The door)

There was preserved

In him

The precious faiblesse

Of life

Peeping through the dam

Of personas

Assigning beauty

Have you ever seen a maple leaf

Fluttering through the air

Soundless, dwelling, passing

On a morning like no other

Any other

Good morning

Light shining through the veins

Revealing a beauty

That gravitates within

A sacrament of nature

A universal humanity in singularity

Singularity plus singularity

Makes for universality

In temporality

Concrete universality

Moves an identity

Into contemporality

Plucked from the tree of life

Poems serve as the guardian of universals

The essence of experience across time

Humanity traced in ink

The potency of the will to free

The mind of men and the mystery of being

Sanctus

Birth marks the Odyssey known to all

Sanctus, sanctus, sanctus

The epic of disordering stories of joys, tears and prayers

So begin the age of wonder and bewilderment

My name is Mephistopheles and I am a misanthrope

Sanctus, sanctus, sanctus

The bird in the sky and the panther on the plain are wise

For their tongue is silent as they go about their business

We are the sons and daughters of trees and hills, not phones and traffic ligh

On my journey, I fold up the earth in a drop of water

To drink every day and cleanse my soul

Like Icarus I long to burn until the sea of pure night consumes me

Sanctus, sanctus, sanctus

Requiem for the living

Mortality as the unmoved mover

In matters of meaning

I read in the sordid book of mortality

Its ink red with the blood of life

The good health of time doctored by the end of ends

Giving birth to the presence of selves

Breathing vitality and vision into their memory and expectation

Dwelling on qualifying reality while in motion

Transitory truth created anew, anew, anew

Mortality is the continuity between life and death

I am a creature who cannot divorce my end

I am a creature at the mercy of the ungovernable flux of moments

Craving for *die Sache selbst* in the family of things

The intentional meaning of the meaningful

Incarnates the engagement of being

The gestalt of experience in becoming, being, am

Summoned by the human condition

Saying out loud that nothing is

But the imagination that moves in our spirit

Passing

Carve no name

When I die

Raise no gravestone

For I have moved on to other

Worlds

Among millions of stars

and millions of names

We are but gusts of questions

Passing

Snowflakes

From the dark unknown above
Crystalized water forms and falls
To the music of heaven and hell
On its lifelong journey to bear witness

Each with a unique texture and testimony
Harmonic yet chaotic, magnificent yet mortal
Flying high and low, swirling with a smile and then a sigh
There is purity in imperfection

The dark soil warmly welcomes each one
And in a silent salute absorbs them
The journey marked now only
By the memory of the earth

About the Poet

Jeanette Bresson Ladegaard Knox is a philosopher, writer and associate professor at the Department of Public Health, the University of Copenhagen, Denmark. She has published translations and numerous articles and books, both non-fiction and fiction.

www.ingramcontent.com/pod-product-compliance
Lightning Source LLC
Chambersburg PA
CBHW032214040426
42449CB00005B/597